The internet revolutionized the world of business, by bringing new technologies and values to the market which soon experienced in amazing growth and private market.

With so many popular companies having been launched thanks to and over the internet, it's no wonder that giants such as Amazon managed to find ways to connect with people and offer them the chance to make a high-end living through certain affiliations and marketing practices, and countless people took the chance and now make over $10,000 a month thanks to these opportunities alone.

As the internet constantly grows, we offer to bring you the current and long-lasting ways anyone can make a solid living with only a computer and network access.

Forget about going to your 9 to 5 job in the morning, forget about your boss or supervisor who constantly blames you for every little detail they consider wrong, and embrace the future of money making through the methods presented and detailed in this book, with carefully selected blueprints to success!!!

Contents

- What is passive income?..4
- Make money like casinos......................................16
- Kindle Direct Publishing - KDP 24
- Drop Shipping..39
- Fulfillment By Amazon – FBA 47
- Youtube..57
- Youtube and Amazon Affiliate Marketing............68
- The Stock Market: 78
- Dividend Paying Stocks.......................................78
- Freelancing 84
- Software Testing..90
- The Millionaire Mindset 91
- Setting goals...92
- The Focus and Multitasking Paradox 102
- Task Priority 109

What is passive income?

Before going into the different ways to make passive income, we have to first cover some information regarding economy and money in general, as regardless of what type of financial success one is following, anyone involved with wealth generating activities is actively playing "the money game".

Businessmen use this term all the time, the money game, because essentially that's what it is. A game in which the player has to generate and sustain as many resources as possible, in order to hit a certain checkpoint of wealth at which the game is won. What's that checkpoint you ask? It depends. For some, that might be just under $1,000,000 while for others it can be as much as $40,000,000 depending on what kind of lifestyle they want to be able to afford without having to work anymore.

Money can be generated in an endless variety of ways, in the XXI. century, almost anything can be turned into profit if we have the right market, which brings us to the next term we need to dissect, market.

Typically, a market, in economic terms, is the fictive place where the powers of supply and demand collide, and trades take place, one changing their supply of a product, for the money of the ones in demand. As the modern world brings so many opportunities, allowing virtually anyone to become wealthy, we no longer have a nominal market for all products in supply and demand relationships, but instead we have specialized markets. Such as a market for stocks, a market for beauty products, etc.

Understanding the particular market you want to actively take place in is essential, as otherwise your product could be in high supply, but there will be no interest directed towards it since you are in the wrong market. Imagine going to the fish market and seeing someone selling a TV. It might be a great working, well priced TV, but all the people at that market are there to buy fish, not electronics. This exaggerated example resembles quite well what happens to products sold in the wrong market.

Let's take some pages to understand how markets actually work. As mentioned, this is where supply and demand are meeting, supply refers to the quantity of product available for sale, while demand is the number of consumers that want to purchase that product, without the balance these two maintain, the markets and economy reach instability, where only the best players can profit.

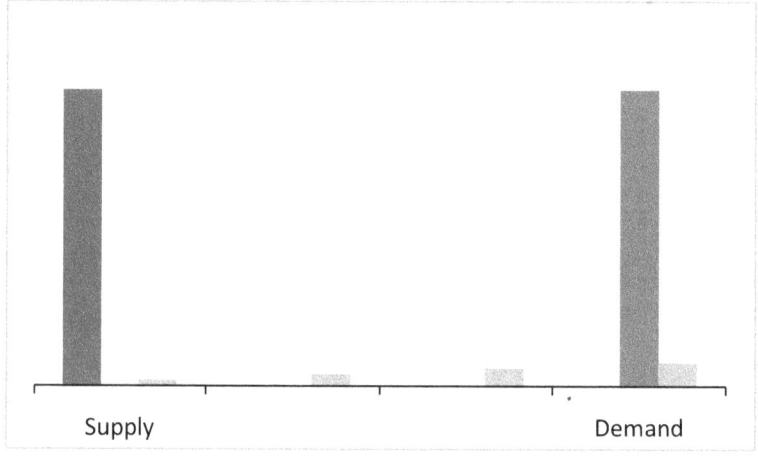

In the real world however, supply and demand never stay the same, as a constant flux hits both elements, impacting the other proportionally.

Naturally, when the supply for a product drops, due to unexpected causes, the demand grows proportionally, because if there were

100 limited edition gold iPhones, and exactly 100 people wanting one of them, the numbers were perfectly proportional. However, if the truck transporting 50 of those phones to a specific store crashes, and its cargo sets on fire, that leaves our supply at 50 phones, for a demand of 100 consumers.

As a consequence, those 100 customers will offer more money to get their hands on one of the phones, as only every second person could get one otherwise. This movement of the market results in the growth of demand, in the shortage of a product's supply.

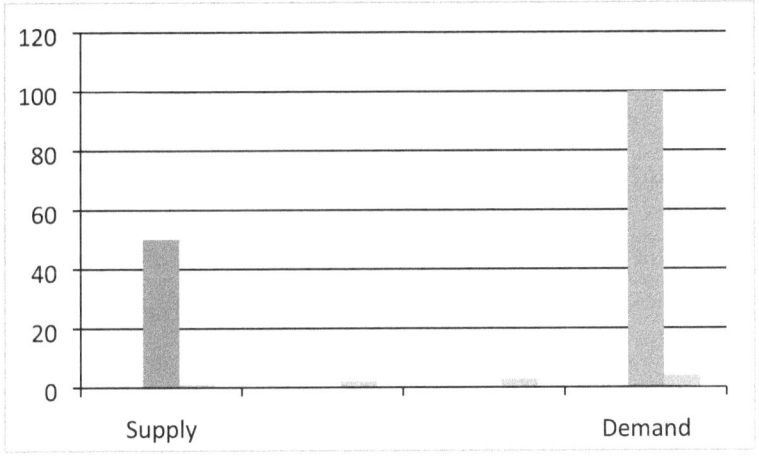

Going the other way, what if the demand drops exponentially? Assuming the newest gaming console will cost around $1,500 and the manufacturers initially put 500,000 units up for sale, estimating off the pre-orders and interest shown that the number of people that will go out and buy one is around half a million, give or take. That would leave us at a proportionate scale, however, a powerful video game development company announces that all of their future games will be available only on PC, and no console will run them. Suddenly the 500,000 enthusiasts no longer rush to buy the console, as they won't be able to play their favorite games on them, so the demand cuts by half.

Usually, during moments like these, companies tend to drop the price of their products, or offer free bonuses with them, in order to drive more customers towards their product to increase demand.

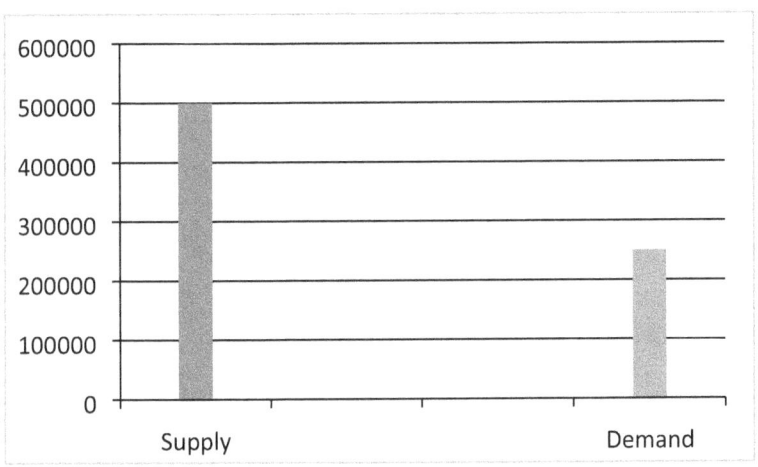

Having talked about supply and demand, to further dissect the markets, we need to discuss the idea of niches. A niche is a subcategory of a specific market, for example, the video game market can be further deconstructed based on genre, such as racing, action, shooting or combat games. All markets have subdivisions, which have to be followed in order to find our target audience.

A game developing company that has been immensely successful with racing games should not use up all resources to quit that niche and enter the combat niche, which is probably dominated by another company, until they have totally exploited the demand for the racing games.

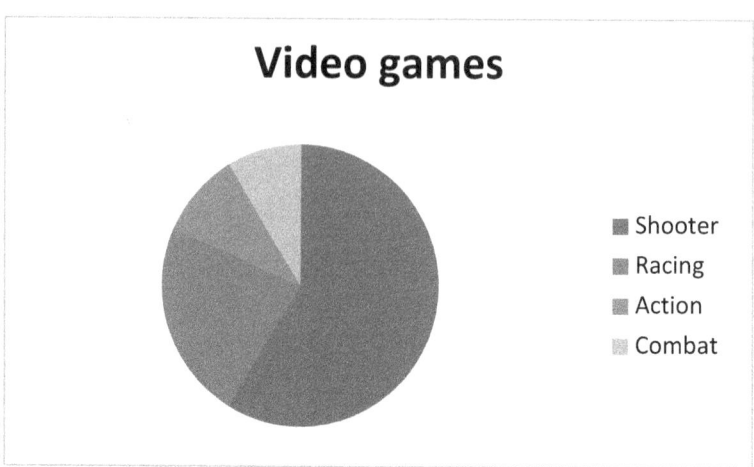

Income types

As types of income, we will talk about active and passive income, as this is probably the most common type of categorization found nowadays.

Active income uses the classic principle of doing something in exchange for something. If you sell your laptop online, and meet the person to make the exchange, he got your laptop while you got their money. The same happens in terms of jobs. We seemingly do not trade anything, instead we work, to get tasks done for the company, and get paid accordingly. According to what? The hourly wage.

So what do we really trade? Only the most valuable resource on the planet, time. An employer buys the employees' time and delegates tasks to them, which they have to accomplish. More on delegation later, but for now, see this business model and understand how time-buying and delegation works in a nutshell:

A bar owner, for example, without a staff, would have the tasks of serving tables, preparing drinks, maintenance, management and security. Impossible to execute all at once, he hires a staff to delegate certain tasks to based on everyone's set of skills. Delegating the task of preparing drinks to bartenders, serving tables to waiters, maintenance and management to a manager and security to a specialized firm.

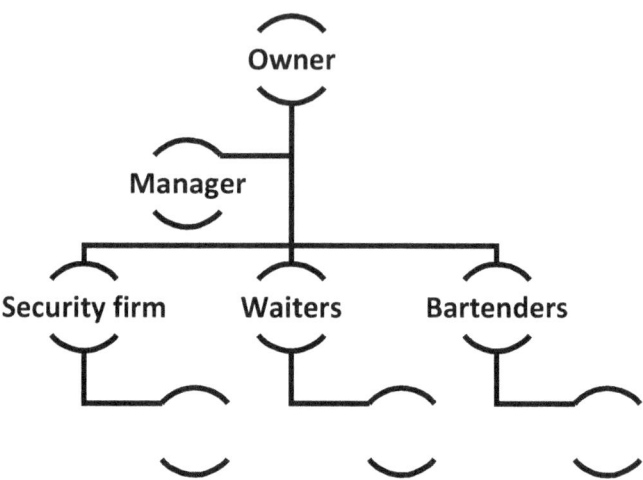

Through this institution, the owner delegates specific tasks to make his or her business functional, as one person cannot take care of all tasks alone. In exchange for the time the staff spends working for him or her, they get paid, **by the hour**, a specific wage.

Money   Time

As the staff cannot work 16 hour shifts, the owner is required to spend twice the amount in order to hire a staff for the second shift, ensuring that his or her business functions 16

hours without drawbacks, so a second exchange happens, with the second shift staff as well.

Money   Time

Ultimately, the owner notices how flourishing the business is, but also how not all tables are served in time, as the staff's productivity is not enough to satisfy the demand of the full bar, so there are two actions to be taken, hiring a fresh staff with higher productivity output, in exchange for a higher wage, or hiring the same quality staff to increase the productivity along the already established staff. Going with the latter, as the same amount of people can hardly satisfy an already overwhelming demand, the owner hires additional people to increase the staffs volume and productivity in order to satisfy all guests and maximize profits.

Money   Time

At the end of the month, the owner pays each staff member their salary based on their hourly wage, as he or she bought their time in order to delegate the necessary tasks in order to ensure the functioning of the bar, pays all other expenses such as the resources used, drinks, appliances, and is left with an amount called profit. It is this profit that determines if the expense of delegating certain tasks to so many people in exchange for the wage was profitable or not, and will make their future decisions based on the monthly profits.

The staff is paid active income, as the trade is time for money, but what should we understand as passive income?

Passive income is essentially wealth generated automatically without having to trade anymore of your time to get it. It can basically make you richer while you sleep or travel, with many entrepreneurs being able to go on an exotic holiday for two weeks and coming home with more money in their bank accounts than they initially left with.

Sounds great, doesn't it? For sure it does, but there is no such thing as a magic formula that will start generating you money instantly, usually instead of trading 40 hours a week to earn a monthly wage, entrepreneurs trade that time and money to create a product or asset that will bring them money each month, without having to put in any more time or money, instead they just collect the money generated by that asset, for which they've spent resources only once. One diamond is a source of passive income.

But how does one create such assets? We are going to cover just that in the Passive Income section of this book.

Make money like casinos

A common saying among businessmen is that you should "make money like casinos", which is the perfect analogy to passive income. To give you a better understanding of the practical analogy of how this works, we'll get into details about casinos now.

Casinos are facilities hosting gambling activities, and are most often found near or in hotels, cruise ships, tourist destinations, etc. Depending on where you live, casinos should not be a rare sight. Casinos always promote themselves as "entertainment facilities" but truth is they are just businesses, meant to bring in profits for the owner. You may be wondering, if casino games all revolve around luck, then how do casinos make money exactly and constantly?

The answer to that question is simple, the casino **always** has an advantage over the average player. There is not one game on the casino floor which has equal odds for both the casino and the player, the casino advantage is also called "**house edge**". Even the most flawless player will lose money, because only winning is impossible.

Making a consistent income out of gambling is only possible if you actually own the casino, or you count cards at blackjack, simply because the mathematics are against you.

Casinos are fun, but they also have an advantage over their players. Small percentages which add up over time and guarantee that the casino will not lose. There are some small secrets which casinos use to get an even bigger advantage and trick players on gambling more money.

1. The casinos' layout is designed to keep players in, using a labyrinth format for most big casinos.

2. Bright and flashy lights and fast music encourage people to gamble at a faster rate

3. The free drinks, especially alcoholic ones will make players lose track of time and money spent in the casino.

4. No windows and clocks in the casino might help you lose track of time.

Everything about casinos is designed to make you play more. Firstly, the free drinks are free for one purpose, make you lose track of how much you've gambled and by getting you dizzy you will completely forget the value of money and are likely to play and bet even more without following a particular strategy, further increasing the house edge over the player. Other free stuff offered by casinos, such as t-shirts, food coupons and souvenirs have the same objective. Making you feel respected, hoping you will return with more cash, because it's no problem giving away $30 worth of items or promotions to players who gamble $150. It's also easy to get lost in the casino atmosphere with the flashy lights, fast sounds and specific perfumes, so stay focused.

Now that you have an idea about why certain things happen, you need to understand something. The most common mistake slot-players make is drinking too much. It's easy to get dizzy with free drinks while playing slot games, but that's exactly what the casino wants you to do. Not only making you lose track of time but also of money, you are prone to gamble more than you can afford and in the meantime drinking more of the free drinks.

Casinos come in two main forms, land-based and online. Land-based casinos have the specific atmosphere while online ones are the most practical, the player being able to gamble from anywhere, on a laptop or even a smartphone.

The common thing between the two is the promotions. Things such as free spins or free credits on sign-up are extremely common online, some of the more popular online casinos won't even ask you to deposit any of your money before giving you some cash to play. Land-based casinos usually offer fidelity cards which in time can grant you 10-20% cash backs or different promotions which will help you in time. Fidelity cards and online promotions should definitely not be ignored, as they are the only true advantage the player can earn from the house.

Now how do we apply this analogy and convert it into a better understanding of business?

First of all, the main concept that brings in money for casinos is the constant edge they have over their players, and giving you the best example would be slot machines. They are programmed to constantly have an advantage, as the chips inside determine how much money they can give out to players while still retaining a profit, this is the mirror image of passive income.

Thinking about this, once a machine is placed in a facility, it starts making money, taking the bets from gamblers and turning them into money for the owner of the casino. That in itself is a stream of passive income, the owner has to pay for that machine and it's setup once, and has to go over some maintenance work only once in a while, during which the machine brings in money constantly, money which once covers the costs of the machine, turns it's intake into profit.

That is the idea of passive income, once an intellectual property is monetized, such as a course or book, it generates money to the owner of those rights or affiliates without having to invest more into the product. The revenue generated by the product, once covering the production costs only generates profit revenues.

Then we have the maintenance work, which for slot machines is a periodic verification of the software, compared to the other passive income sources, this matches the maintenance work a landlord has to do over their real estate to ensure its correct conditions and value.

The promotion cards ran by casinos are the equivalent of email lists for businesses, to solidify contact with the market. A gambler that gets a promotion card is more likely to go back to that exact casino, just like a person shopping for shoes would rather go to the store they have offers at, even if the amount dropped through the card is almost irrelevant, the facility can further grasp on to the consumer of their product.

The last big match in terms of business and casinos is how the gambling facilities are always offering something extra, such as a free meal or drinks, sometimes even show tickets, with passive income, offering something for free is great in order to get people to buy your actual product, such as a free demo of a course or app. Before going forward and talking about the ways one can generate passive income, it's important to know that all businessman have more than one strain of income, so limiting yourself to just one of the following sources would be foolish, instead, opt to build an empire like this.

Kindle Direct Publishing - KDP

Generating passive income through the internet is more than just simple, anyone with access to the global platform can do it in a variety of ways, as the internet connects billions of people, making it easy for a supplier to reach potential customers in demand, so without further to do, let's get into the passive ways you can generate income through the internet, starting with royalties.

This is the first type of passive income I had come into contact with and started earning money with when I was about 14 years old. Having just started high school, I went through what I now call "the magician phase", when I would constantly harass my classmates with magic tricks, but with time, comes improvement, and my skills got pretty good. The summer after my freshman year of high school, I found a platform that allowed magicians to sell their own magic tricks. This meant that I someone had just come up with an idea for a trick and has an original method, that method could be sold online over their website.

After writing an email to the company, they agreed to give me a space on their platform, and out of sheer enthusiasm, I called the camera man I met during a talent show in between high schools who really like magic and he shot the trailer for my magic trick. He refused to accept any money saying he did it just to help me achieve success in magic, a man that I will always be in debt to. In about a week the trailer was ready and I filmed a tutorial revealing the secret to the trick with my cellphone, and pretty soon, the trick was online and ready to be purchased.

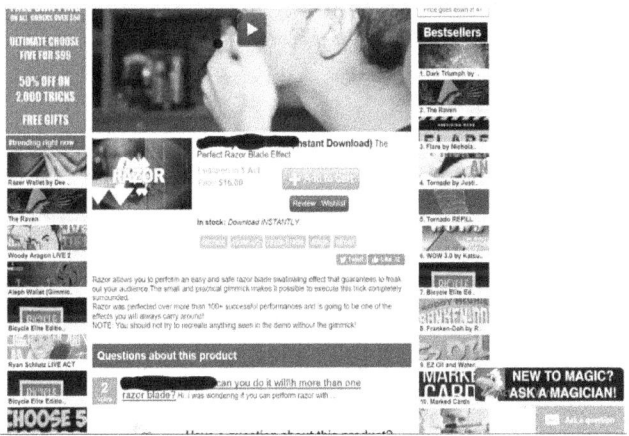

As expected, it did not do well on the website, as not many people would spend $20 on a magic trick that shows you how to eat razor blades, presented by a 14 year old blabbing English. It did however sell enough copies to generate about $400, and that was enough to prove me that on the internet, anyone can make money. If a 14 year old could make $400 on the internet, without having to work more than the 2 hours it took to shoot the trailer and the tutorial, anyone could make it, which brings us here, royalties.

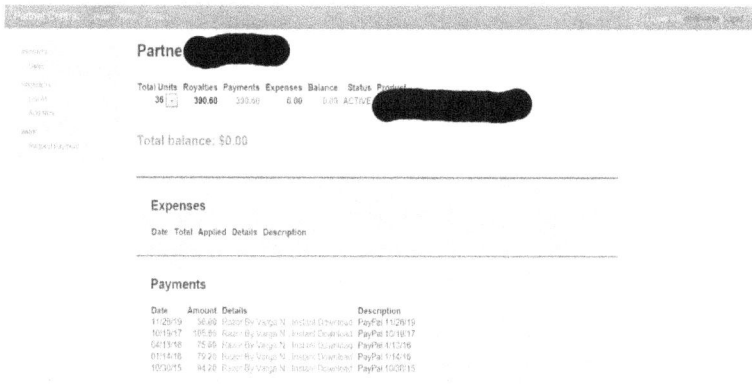

For anyone unfamiliar with the concept, royalties are the percentage of a product's price that you get after selling one unit on the hosting platform. In that case, I got 70% of the price of the product, for each individual sell, and as for the big names on the market, making a million dollars over the course of one year through royalties is a reality.

That however was regarding magic, not a market most people are able to create a product in, so now let's shift our focus to how anyone can make passive income through the internet, starting with the number one platform in terms of ease and practicality, Amazon's Kindle Direct Publishing or KDP for short.

Amazon hit the ebook market hard by purchasing Kindle, the company holding most of the world around ebooks, and with the launch of Kindle Direct Publishing, the platform used to publish this book too.

Essentially Amazon allows people to write an ebook, design a cover, write a description, price it, and then sell it on their platform. This massive idea opened a brand new market for individual self-publishers whom couldn't previously launch their works for free, to finally release their intellectual property.

The same as with the magic trick I had been selling, for every ebook sale I make on Amazon, I get a percentage of that product's price for myself. While ebooks are a low-value product, Amazon also offers the opportunity to create paperback products, which rank a lot better in terms of payment. Even so, today there are publishers who earn over $10,000 a month off ebook and book royalties, and the formula to that level of passive income is not as complicated as you'd expect.

When it comes to KDP, publishers have two routes to choose from, becoming a publisher or a self-publisher. Self-publishers are people that write their books themselves, just as I am writing this one, while a publisher would hire an individual, known as a ghost writer, to do the work for him, and in exchange, the writer will be paid for the book. The publisher sets the book on the market under their own name, and collects the revenues off it.

We will not cover the standard publishing process, as Amazon offers explanatory videos on that topic and the process itself is not that complicated, instead, we will focus on how to actually make an extra profit off KDP to start your first potential passive income stream.

First and foremost you should decide which path fits your capacity best, investing in books to be written by ghostwriters, or save the money and write the book yourself? Here is a dilemma most people try to solve the wrong way. Most books issued by publishers and self-publishers are non-fiction books, writings which can be done on virtually any topic and do not require a strong fantasy and literature thinking. In this book we will be focusing on things anyone can do to create passive income streams, and literary works are not in the capabilities of everyone.

Sticking with non-fiction, one should accept the idea that a strong book, at maxed out potential will cost around $500, including the cover, the ebook and the paperback, formatting into audiobook format and having a strong description written. This is the publisher's way of doing business, basically having a writing company do the work of writing the book and turning it into paperback and kindle format, and hiring freelancers to inexpensively create a cover and write a product description that sells. This plus an additional $50 to have the book converted into an audiobook. After this process, the total investment should be around $500, for three products that will become income generating assets (the ebook, audiobook, and paperback) and professional made covers. With that in mind, for the course of its lifetime, that book will produce income to the publisher repeatedly, so even if it takes the products three months to generate the initial $500 back, after those three months every cent generated is pure profit.

By far the most important thing when publishing is the niche research, remembering what we've discussed earlier about supply and demand. Topics such as cook-books and dog-training books bring in a lot of money, but since the money was so good initially, thousands of publishers released books on those topics, and now the market is oversaturated. The supply became much greater than the demand. So what do we recommend?

Finding a market and shrinking the search-terms down. Even if the cook-book market was oversaturated, we can further deconstruct that market on smaller niches, such as keto or paleo diet based cook-books, topics that have yet to be addressed in such volume, and there is still money around them.

For the self-publisher who would rather not spend money but chooses to write him or herself, the costs of the book are cut drastically, because all you need is a professional cover, something that freelancers can nail for 5-10 bucks. For anyone hesitant of trying KDP because of the costs of the simple publisher and are afraid to start writing, do give it a shot. The system is very simple, Amazon does a great job explaining its mechanisms to new publishers, and also comes with a great advantage. Amazon is the biggest platform out there, with hundreds of millions of credit cards linked to the website, so once your target audience finds your products, it's extraordinary easy to buy them.

    The description is what sells the book, along-side the cover, so no money should be cut off for those major elements. A fresh publisher can get about two books out a month, without writing excessively, and once those books generate enough revenue, the next step is to transition from being a self-publisher, to just publishing the works of other ghostwriters you've hired, as that is the main step towards the automatization of your business.

    Each month ordering 3 books from various writing companies, 3 covers and 3 descriptions, along with the request for audiobook formatting takes one hour twice a week, one hour to place the orders and one hour to publish the three books once your products are ready, a simple process that allows many to generate five figures monthly, and to keep that number increasing by ordering more and more books each month, to increase the number of passive income strains owned by the publisher.

The only real work is finding three niches to publish in, based on the sales ranks of the first 5 books that pop-up after searching for a keyword.

If the sales ranks of all 5 books are under 100,000 and no strong characters show up with books with 200+ reviews, the market is good to go.

This is by far the easiest way one can get familiar with passive income, as it is virtually free, and all of the required educational material can be found on Amazon.

So how exactly do you start earning significant money?

The first step is to create your first product, either by writing the book yourself or hiring someone to do it, either through a freelancer or a writing company. The next steps are going to be determined by your approach, so if you want to hire people to write your product, you can move on to the next paragraph, if you are opting to write your book yourself instead, keep reading. Before jumping recklessly into it, consider three things, one, if you have the necessary skill for writing? It may not sound too intimidating, and it's not, if you have your grammar and comfort in check. Secondly, choosing a topic, you can't really write about anything, as the lack of personal knowledge about the subject will lower the quality of your book, a general set of skills or information in the niche you are working with will be required to make sure your product has a high enough quality, and third, if there is money in that market. The latter will be discussed in the following paragraph.

So you are all set, you have made your decision and are ready to make money, what's next? Choosing a profitable niche. Some people underestimate the importance of a strong niche, which leads them to a path of unprofitable products. First and foremost, have a topic you like or think is profitable.

Then, check if it is. Search for it on Amazon's book store, and see if the first five books that show up have a sales rank of under 100,000. If at least four out of five books have that, the niche is likely to be profitable.

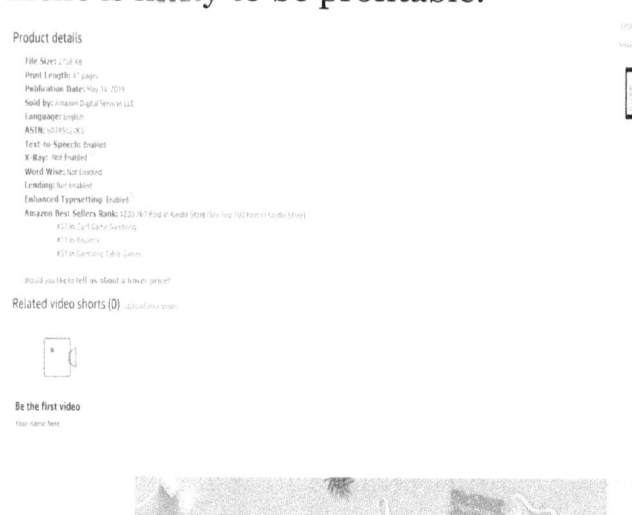

A red flag in terms of niche selection is the presence of strong authority figures. People whose book shows up in the first five results, and has a sales rank of under 20,000 and more than 200 reviews. Problem is, those products are just too strong on the market, with consumers opting to buy those instead of others' books, since the information it offers is backed up by the reviews.

Once that is determined, have the product made, either by writing it yourself or by having it ordered. How long should a book be? A minimum of 7,000 words is recommended, with no top limit. 10,000 – 20,000 is a more than solid area to work with, depending on how vast the subject is.

After having your product written, comes the most important part after the market choice, cover design and description writing. Both can be done by yourself, but, a strong cover costs little, freelancers are constantly taking orders for cover design, so their market is so competitive, with the spike in supply, the price is more than affordable. A dynamic, big text cover is advised, with an image or subjectivity that captures the interest of your consumers. Most freelancers will design a great cover without much effort, but it's worth mentioning how one should know their direct audience and the cover should be made to that audience's liking. For instance a book on the subject of binge eating, has a direct audience of women aged 20-40, and that should be taken into consideration when designing the cover. Here we have an example of a good quality cover image for an ebook.

The next big pillar of ebook publishing is the description. If you have a product, with a high quality cover, people will be clicking on it. That's when the last big element comes into play, as the description is what actually sells the product. A good description, offering detailed information on the contents, and showcasing the value of your product is what's going to get people to hit the "buy" button.

With all that being said, one last detailed look at the core of ebook publishing, the option of creating 3 products in one, with paperbacks and audiobooks on the horizon. Audiobooks are the fastest growing way people consume information right now, and are most likely to take over the business, so having your books converted to paperback, as well as audiobooks a concept worth noting.

After having your first book released, focus onto turning the profits earned, into new books for further expansion of the business. Each new book means 2 or 3 additional passive income sources, which in time add up to create a massive revenue spring to feed your bank account. Most publishers do not succeed in their first few attempts, so multiple books should be released onto the market to see and test what works and what does not, at the moment you are reading this.

Drop Shipping

This is the future of commerce, known as e-commerce, where the buyer can order a product from the distributor, who never even touches the product, instead, he/she buys the product from the supplier for much less, has the supplier shipping it, while the distributor takes the difference as profit. The origins of this practice come from the late 2000s, when people would set up a domain listing many products, and whenever an order was placed, that domain owner would just order the product from a supplier for way less, and ask the supplier to ship the product to the address of the buyer, expressly asking them not to place the receipt in the package, but instead the domain owner would send a virtual one.

This process, although profitable, was heavily flawed. First of all, the domain's owner would need to hire someone to code and design a retail website for them, a service that was regarded as expensive during these times.

Secondly, the release of a receipt from an unauthorized individual was also facing legal issues, since the supplier had the legal obligation of emitting a receipt, while the one running this drop shipping business through them, would ask them to do quite the opposite, to keep the consumer from knowing the actual price of the product.

Finally, it was quite a lot of work. Not only that the entrepreneur had to run the whole operation manually, the publishing and marketing of their products had to be done in a manner that made it difficult to draw traffic to their page, and get a significant number of sales, unless they marketed the perfect product in the perfect place.

As an additional note, shipping would also represent a problem sometimes, since the Asian retailers who would supply the products needed more than 2 weeks to ship the orders to certain parts of the world, which made it incredibly difficult to manage all orders and still have them delivered in time.

As time went on and people started to see the potential in such businesses, multiple platforms started offering entrepreneurs the opportunity to drop ship products easily, with all of the issues listed above having been fixed. These platforms would sometimes offer free domains, easy to set-up templates for retail businesses, and most important of all, the chance to affiliate yourself with bigger names in the retail industry.

Don't see the value yet? Well, if you are skeptic about having to manage all of those orders, asking the companies not to include a receipt, etc. now, these platforms take care of it for you. The drop shipper has to do only three things: setting-up, creating the line of products, marketing.

After that, the only active work that needs to be done is the constant refreshing of the marketing strategies, as on the e-commerce business, marketing and advertising is a lot different from traditional practices, as a new age dawns for technology, so does for business.

Assuming you have chosen a platform to operate on, (we do not make any direct recommendations as we do not support or receive sponsorships for any particular ones) depending on their offers, costs, etc. It's time to set up. What the goal really is when setting up is to create a brand for yourself, with the adequate color, font, and image layout.

Imagine a retail store that works with rock and roll items, bracelets, t shirts, bandanas, etc. We cannot have a page that is all pink and showcasing images of rivers and coal mines, instead, a palette of color associated with the rock theme is more adequate, such as black, red, white and grey.

Now, think about who the target audience might be? This is why it's recommended that you start off with something you are interested in, it's easier to determine such factors if you can ask the person you know best, yourself, what would you like from a store to make you buy from it?

In terms of the products you'd like, do not include every item that every such store has, otherwise you will become a lately established copy of another brand. Instead, opt for something new, new designs for bracelets, new t shirt designs, new decorative items such as posters, having a unique selection of products will make you stand out and draw traffic to your online business.

Setting up and adding the line of items is childishly easy with modern platforms that include introductive videos that break down every step of the process, except for the third installment, marketing. The advertising is what sets profitable and non-profitable drop shippers apart from each other.

Traditionally, advertising used to be done in the physical world, with banners, logos and projections, but when it comes to e-commerce, the advertisement has to be done through the increasingly popular e-advertisement, as a store that only exists in the virtual realm can only be marketed in that same field.

When most people hear about online advertising they first think about Facebook ads, a truly powerful marketing weapon, but in the case of drop shipping, there is a major issue, the costs. Most readers will be looking forward to start earning money passively with little to no investments required, and Facebook ads can be expensive, especially since you are trying to market a product internationally to maximize sales potential.

Then how do we find an inexpensive marketing strategy to bind all three elements together? Quite surely, we've all heard of the people that aren't great at anything, aka. influencers, well, to some extent, the least expensive and most effective strategy is to have Instagram pages with a strong follower-base advertise for you, counter-cost.

Not all pages are created equal, so now let's try to determine a pattern that leads to profitable advertisements.

As a first disclaimer, avoid pages that have too many followers, whenever we are talking about millions, or over 500k for that matter, their follower-base is already too vast to be suitable for a drop shipping store's advertisement. Sticking to an interval of above 50,000 to 250,000 at most, will have the best chance to offer you a profitable advertising platform, as the people following those pages may still belong to practically similar social categories. (you'll see where I'm going in a minute)

Now you must focus on the relationship between your product and the potential followers of a page. For a rock and roll accessories and merchandise store, an Instagram page dedicated to rockers will be most suitable. If your products revolve around cats for example, such as t shirts with cat prints, mugs, bracelets, fluffy ears, etc. then the primary consumers could be found following a page dedicated to cat videos and photos, or a page for a single cat, such as Dan Bilzerian's.

Lastly we need to negotiate the price for a shout-out. Most influencers haven't yet worked with drop shippers, while some have, so a price for a 24h promotional story with a link in the description, on a page with over 100,000 followers, should be around $100. Plus-minus that is a fair price, and as a refined detail, do not address influencers that constantly do these shout-outs, instead try to find some that rarely promote sponsored items. For smaller pages, sometimes $50 or just a few free products will be enough to get your store or product linked to their account for 24 hours through a story.

As final tips for anyone looking forward to start a drop shipping business:
- Include both commonly available products you see on well-performing shops
- Do not hesitate to open more shops with different specific themes, expanding your field of work increases potential sales times the amount
- Do spend the $40 asked by Amazon to list your products on their platform, they

are the biggest giant in the online retail industry
- Use the profits generated by drop shipping to fund investments on your KDP business, and vice-versa. Turning the short-term profits from one business to long-term revenue from another creates stability in your finances and helps boost and improve further businesses and income sources.

Fulfillment By Amazon – FBA

Tying into our previous topic, Fulfillment By Amazon or FBA as it's commonly known is vastly similar to modern drop shipping but brings the whole game to another level.

The giant of e-commerce we know today created the same option other platforms did, but with a huge addition. Having your products sold directly by Amazon, through their fantastic logistics and marketing, sales can hit mind-blowing levels.

According to Amazon's annual report, in 2018, about 200,000 ordinary people working through FBA made an income of over $100,000 from the comfort of their home, and a whopping 25,000 broke the 1 million dollars milestone in the same year.

The biggest problem is that people still do not understand or at least believe how massive FBA is and how much money can be generated through that platform. If 200,000 people could pull in six figures, anyone can. Not only that but the fundamental mistake most ordinary people still make is refusing to accept how big e-commerce is and would rather skip out of opportunities like this.

How is it different from regular drop shipping?

1. It's undeniably the biggest platform you could launch your product on, with no considerable competitors.
2. More than half of the products sold by Amazon in 2018 came from individuals working with FBA from their computers, so if you've had two orders from Amazon last year, odds are, someone made a nice profit off your purchase.
3. Amazon does almost everything for you, such as shipping, packaging and delivery, so the products your customers receive come under the Amazon label. So noticeably, your market is not going to be an audience redirected off social media platforms, but instead, the biggest market out

there on the virtual realm, with millions of active buyers on a daily basis.
4. It has world-wide range, so regardless of where you live, you can start selling on Amazon right away, with no issue, since you never come into contact with the products.

How it works?

Sadly this is the part where most of you might lose interest, but I strongly suggest you don't. In a nutshell, Amazon allows individuals to sell their products on their platform and split the money, however, you need to first purchase the product, instead of having it automatically purchased whenever an order is placed.

Since Amazon has a 24h delivery policy for certain countries, they cannot have a product ordered from the manufacturer the day an order is placed on their platform, meaning that you, as an affiliate, have to buy a stock of that product, that you pay for with your own money, in order to ship that stock to an Amazon warehouse.

Before losing all hope, keep in mind that manufacturers offer huge discounts for products when bought in big quantities, such as 100 pieces or more. This can make a mug that you sell on Amazon for $15 cost you only a mere $1 or less, and the beautiful thing is, Amazon offers an infinite variety of products, so anything from kitchen hardware to children's books etc. can be sold on Amazon because there is constant demand. Products such as a magnetic knife holder for your kitchen could cost you only $1 to buy from Alibaba, the store you would be purchasing your items from, but can easily be sold on Amazon to the average consumer for $25.

The next major advantage, if it weren't obvious, is how you get free traffic. No need to contact influencers or buy Facebook ads, because there is literally not a single platform bigger than Amazon's when it comes to the e-commerce business, so the costs of buying shout-outs are completely eliminated.

We are not going into details about FBA and the set-up phase, as there is no virtual need for it, since Amazon has produced some great content for explanatory purposes so anyone can understand how everything works in great detail, and we highly suggest watching those. But we do feel the need to talk about what products are the most profitable and why, so this is where we're heading.

Scanning in time for potential products is essential since you have to determine multiple factors before investing your money into buying a stock of 100 units on your own risk. Risk isn't really a good term, as the potential risk factor in FBA is quite low, most products will sell decently not because of how great they are, but because the demand on Amazon is constantly stable for all products due to its size.

The first factor you should consider is the cost. How much will one unit cost you if you buy 100? Generally speaking we'd advise $1 or less for products that will be sold on Amazon for less than $20, and $2 for products that range around $35-$40. A product you can sell for $35 and costs only $1 is a great sign of high potential profit. To determine how much your product can be sold for later, do a market research on similar product, taking a decorative "Star Wars" poster as an example, if you see lots of products matching that description selling for $15 or $20, you can't really price yours at $30 but shouldn't be going bellow $15. Keep in mind how your product needs to stand out, so do not ship items that are already common. If you find lots of classic posters and vintage art, try something new, find posters with caricatures or themed after another tv show combined with Star Wars to form a new product, this way anyone who want a typical poster will have to choose between the hundreds of similar ones, or yours, and everyone who wants a unique piece for their wall will have to go with the design you are selling, since it's out of the ordinary.

    Secondly, make sure to avoid seasonal products. Indeed Halloween decorations make a killing during late September and October, but after that, interest in such products drops significantly, since their sole purpose has expired for that year. Sending a stock of decorations in early September to a warehouse can earn you a significant profit for the next moth to come, but the stock shouldn't exceed 100 units, because otherwise you will be left with them until next year. Seasonal products sell great during their time if the product is unique enough on an already saturated market, but is not worth the resources to be commercialized year-round. Be on the watch for trends too, since sudden spikes in a certain video game's popularity, or a TV show's rating and viewers can mean in increase in the demand to themed products. The fidget spinner was an enormous trend a few years ago, and the smartest and fastest entrepreneurs made a quick killing during the craze, selling cheap spinners with intricate and unique designs for enormous profits.

    Lastly, be on the lookout for products that go as great gifts. Since the Amazon return policy could mean an issue for products that come from Alibaba and are very low on quality, without you ever touching the product, the best way to get around this issue is to work with gift-able items.

    When is the last time you've returned a gift to the store? And if it happened recently, how often has that happened in the past? Exactly. People do not return gifts for a variety of reasons, which can act as a shield against the return policy, and also be a constant market, since people celebrate their birthdays every day of the year.

Contrary to what some may think, FBA is probably the strongest and most accessible source of passive income one can generate. Indeed, you will need to make an investment, and claims range from anywhere from $300 to $4000 in order to have a strong starting position, truth of the matter is, $1000 is more than enough if you calculate your moves correctly. Research tools for all sorts of markets exist, both for the book market, for the regular products market, etc. but we are not going to reveal any names because we do not want to associate our work with any other company, feel free to check out these research tools by simply running a quick search on the internet and without a doubt you will stumble upon multiple names for each of these passive income sources, and are free to further investigate which one to get. Research tools are a powerful weapon in any businesses arsenal and getting one is highly recommended, they save up lots of time and money since most of these software are one-time purchase products with lifetime licensing and free updates.

A classic business takes upwards from $10,000 to start, without mentioning the time, staff and physical effort needed to run the enterprise after it has settled its place on the market, along with monthly advertisement costs and marketing, putting that into perspective when considering one or two thousand dollars in order to start a fully functional service that generates six figures for over 200,000 people and even allows 25 THOUSAND people to make over a million dollars a year, FBA is by far the better choice.

If the issue for you is money and are not willing to risk a loan, we highly suggest trying another cost-free method of earning the money needed, such as KDP. With that in mind, we will be moving forward to our next topic, and the last one to revolve around

Amazon Affiliate Marketing Program or Amazon Affiliate Program as it is now called.

Youtube

It is well known by now how Youtube pays its content creators well, from thousands of youtubers having a net worth of over $1 million, it comes as no surprise that more and more people are trying to get in on the business.

There are many pros regarding Youtube but there is also a new major con, which we will be discussing in a few pages.

The beauty of Youtube stands in the enormous reach they have, being the biggest and most popular video streaming network, and with such great resources comes great money, something that allowed young individuals to gross millions by recording quality content from the comfort of their home and by simply being themselves.

What makes this platform so attractive to many is that no matter what you are interested in, and what type of channel you'd want to start, there is a consumer base for you. From people playing videogames to vloggers and people who simply record themselves while gambling, a solid subscriber base can be developed through consistency and dedication.

However we're not here to discuss how amazing this platform is to achieve fame and notoriety, we want to find out where all of that money lies.

First and foremost, Youtube doesn't allow you to make money right away. First your channel has to meet certain requirements, which, as of this writing are having 1,000 subscribers and 4,000 hours of watch time in the past 12 months. Keep in mind that Youtube is constantly changing policies and monetization terms and conditions, so as of you reading this, the data written in this paragraph could be outdated.

Meeting those requirements is not that difficult if one creates a solid content material and uploads constantly, but it still takes some time and effort, sometimes even money if hiring an editor is necessary.

Then we have the most basic monetization method, ads. To put it simply, you allow Youtube to put ads at the beginning of your video, which can usually be skipped after a few seconds, that enables the monetization of your video, depending on the number of views, as one article reads:

"If it's a CPC advertisement, then you get paid based on how many viewers click on the ads surrounding your video. Per view, advertisers on average pay $.18. If your channel receives 1,000 views, it's worth $18. Google keeps 45 percent of what is made, so a YouTuber would make (on average) $9.90 per 1,000 views."

We could talk endlessly about how Youtube operates, but becoming a professional youtuber and earning vast amounts of money out of this exclusively takes a lot of time. Although one can get filthy rich through this platform, that will require the primary goal to be fame, motivating them to pursue posting higher quality content, more consistently and to climb the ladder of fame on Youtube. Most people that want to generate solid passive income and get rich do not look forward to Youtube because it simply consumes too much time and the rate of growth can be extremely slow unless they manage to become one of the isolated cases that reaches a level of controversy which enables their channel to grow rapidly.

If becoming a famous Youtuber is your goal, be aware that you can easily make a living out of it, however that will require a long time, overall we do recommend this platform for reaching virtual fame, but we'd also advise you to read the last paragraph of this section as it discussed the issues that the new GDPR system brings for the future.

Monetarily speaking Youtube is great for one sole purpose, having a fan-base. It is the single best and most powerful advertising an individual can achieve. Having that big of a reach, marketing becomes both free and effective, just remember when was the last time you watched your favorite content creator's videos and suddenly at the middle or end of the video, the start mentioning a brand?

Probably happened recently. Having a platform of your own with a strong base of followers is amazing bait for both established and starting companies to advertise their products, especially since most such companies will target audiences linked to the type of content that person creates. Skin care, grooming and fashion items are commonly seen to be advertised in style and trend videos, while gaming equipment is often provided to the gamers by the companies themselves in exchange for advertising.

These deals can take many different forms, depending on the size of the channel and the amount of videos they put out, relative to the number of subscribers and rate of growth. Smaller channels may only receive free products from the company to be featured and used by the creator, which already shows the benefits of owning strong media channels. Smaller name youtubers that make content on style might receive a full set of clothing from different brands just to be mentioned in their videos, which in itself is value, adding that to the revenue generated by the ads system and being a youtuber is not as bad as some may think.

Bigger channels receive stronger sponsorships as well, which come in the form of affiliations and can generate a limitless amount of money. Usually a brand propose a deal where the content creator gets a special link for a certain product, then in a few future videos, the creator has to feature and advertise the product, usually aggressively, to get people to buy it, "using the special link in the description bellow", we all have heard that phrase before. That special link in indeed special, because although it may offer a small deal, such as 15% off, for every purchase done through that link or by using a code provided by the creator, they also receive their cut of the price.

    This can best be seen with fashion channels, where nearly all videos have a sponsor and a special link. Imagine how much money can a creator generate when they have hundreds of videos, all featuring products from about 10-15 brands, and with every purchase made through their link or code, money is generated, along-side the base income from video views.

    Going one step further, we will now understand why Youtubers make so much money. Most content creators will also have a product of their own, such as a book, clothing line, skin care products, videogames or special courses. Books are the most common item that these people "make", although most of them are created through ghostwriters and strong publishing companies.

Do you see the connection yet? If not, please start reading the book from the beginning until you do.

Having a product of your own, as well as a fan-base that consumes your content on a regular basis is the easiest and by far the best way to advertise your own products. Whenever a youtuber launches a book, a few weeks later it is labeled as a bestseller, and not because of the greatness of that book, but thanks to the fans that buy the item as memorabilia or simply to support the content creator, boosting the popularity of that book then makes it more likely to pop-up in other people's searches which have nothing to do with the youtuber, but since the book is so heavily reviewed with positivity and is in such high popularity, even more people will buy it.

There is an easily noticeable pattern when it comes to Youtube channnles:

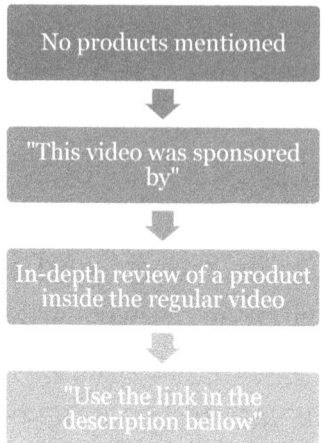

Once the whole development is over, an established youtuber has multiple streams of passive income flowing in:

1. Video Ad Revenue

2. Free Sample Products

3. Affiliate Links

4. Promo Codes

5. And most importantly free marketing for their own products

We have purposefully left Amazon Affiliate Marketing aside until now because we wanted to first break down the system used by youtubers to make such revenue and how / why it works.

Nearly the same opportunities shine upon regular bloggers as well, but their number is scarcer, with the digitalization of the modern world, video is perhaps the most convenient way to consume information, most people would rather watch a video about a topic than read an article about the same size on that subject, as we are getting more and more comfortable as a species, innovation brings value, and that value should be exploited for as long as it can. Probably until 2025 the gold rush of internet money making sources is going to be flourishing, but eventually the market will settle and saturate, leaving only the established power figures unharmed. Before moving on, we will also address the power of Instagram influencers since the growing popularity of the social media platform created a spike in young people inspiring to become professional influencers.

Without making fun of this rather stupid concept and despite wanting to dismiss the existence of such a profession, it seems like the direction we're moving towards as a society will unavoidably lead to the word "influencer" being the equivalent of what TV hosts were to our grandparents.

Being an Instagram influencer does, without a doubt have potential, with paid shout-outs being popularized by other businesses, and the number paid sponsorships from famed companies rising like never before, however we want to warn you about one major risk factor.

Social media platforms have always been a subject of aging, and ultimately forgetting. Myspace, Hi5 and Yahoo Messenger are just a couple of names that once ruled the common conception of the idea of the internet, but now have long been forgotten.

Some current giants are perhaps going to survive the test of time, as the scale at which they developed is alarmingly high, thanks to the spread of the internet the strongest platforms have over 3 billion users, but how much until the future generations develop the next big thing?

It can be 10 years from now, 25 years from now, or perhaps just a couple of months from now we will see the launch of a new social media platform that will grow even bigger than the current giants.

Be aware of that if you were interested in such money making routines, since the risk of losing your market is not just possible, it is highly probable, an account with 3 million followers could perhaps only raise 500,000 on the new platform where fresh faces will gain popularity faster than the already established ones on "outdated-to-be" platforms, so the longevity of such an activity is highly doubted.

Youtube and Amazon Affiliate Marketing

AAM or Amazon Affiliate Marketing is one of the easiest methods for media personalities to make money, because the income is truly passive, with very little work needed in order to have a continuous stream of revenue flowing in.

Affiliate Marketing overall works similarly to the advertisement we've talked about earlier, with youtubers, but instead of having companies reach out and offer deals for notoriety figures with special links and codes, you have to apply for a marketing affiliation, with few criteria to pass. More details about the program can be found on Amazon's dedicated page, and filling pages by copying their data would not be a great idea. To give you a brief overview, Amazon basically pays you to advertise their products, through special links dedicated to your affiliate page. When someone buys a product through your links, Amazon gives you a commission over the price.

Every year thousands of people make incredible amounts of money through these commissions, this alone enabling them to cover their daily costs and make a great living out of affiliate marketing alone, but it has to be done wisely, how wisely? Let us answer that.

The best way to let you have the full image is to compare this to the previous section's "link in the description bellow" paragraphs. At first glance, the obvious benefit is the open door Amazon has for anyone to try their luck with affiliate marketing, instead of having to wait desperately for companies to reach out to you. Indeed it first may seem appealing, but the truth is, the amount of money earned through affiliate marketing is not the greatest, ranging somewhere between three and four percent as of this writing. Do not lose faith just yet, after breaking down the infrastructure of the system we will talk about the profitable ways this affiliation can make solid money.

Second of all, Amazon doesn't enforce any advertising obligations, you can try marketing that product as much as you'd like, as it is meant to work for nearly everyone.

Another key difference is that unlike the companies reaching out to you, the type of products you can advertise are not tailored for your content type, meaning that one platform that revolves around travel or gaming videos can easily pocket money off anything if done properly.

Here you could notice the imbalance, the market you get to work with is bigger, although not all products are fitting for your audience, regardless of the limitless options you get, but the commission is significantly smaller. Including the affiliate link to a $15 book to your video's description will bring you less than one dollar. The solution to this issue might be unpredicted by some yet obvious to others, you have to sell expensive items.

The world of business is not kind, and when the goal is to make money, selling items that might be too expensive for some to buy should not be a problem as long as there are people willing to pay that price.

We will give you a strong example of what Amazon Affiliate Marketing done right looks like before moving on and breaking down the steps to accumulate that same wealth.

Example:

A youtuber, we will not give names for this example, as it is not in the interests of our readers, made amazing travel vlogs. He had great skills in the fields of video editing, so the scenes in his videos were great to look at.
Naturally, travel items are not necessarily expensive, but the hardware used to shoot those scenes is.

Our example linked the camera, tripod, lenses, and other hardware used to shoot his videos in such great quality with affiliate links to his videos. We are looking at cameras that cost over $300, where even the low commission rate turns into a hefty sum if purchased by multiple people. This guy raised a great amount of money through the affiliate links he had along-side the basic revenue from Youtube, which is exactly what you're looking for.

Amazon's affiliate links do require a platform for you to advertise the products to the masses with, such as a video or blogging space, but if you have been convinced to start a Youtube channel for advertisement purposes, we will offer you the insight to what you need to know when starting such a project and how to monetize it efficiently.

Before all, you will require a platform, with Youtube being the biggest one on the market, it's perhaps best to go with the video streaming giant, then of course, launching and growing a channel. The subject of the channel should be up to you, going with something that makes up one of your genuine interests, it could be money, videogames, film and television, comedy, etc. basically all types of content have a market on Youtube.

Growing that channel is going to take some time, as a primary weapon you have consistency in uploads and quality content. Not everyone is experienced or even familiar with video editing, but thankfully thousands of instructional videos can be found online teaching about video editing for Youtube content creators. Learning a new skill is beneficial nonetheless so do not hesitate to get into some software knowledge.

As the channel grows, at one time you will experience the monetization of your videos, by crossing the threshold required to start running ads, money will already start flowing in. Once that is achieved, the process will jumpstart. That money can be reinvested into hiring an editor and thus outputting higher quality content and saving some time that was usually spent editing.

Once the process is getting automated, forming a brand-name is starting to become a priority, color schemes, logos, brand names, and a generic topic that will stand at the core of your content have to be grown into the channel, based on the feedback received over time on the previous videos.

As your channel starts to look professional, you can start running these affiliate ads, but we need to find the right products.

The general rule is to stay away from products that are under $1000, such as expensive cameras, VR gear, phones, and other high-end tech gear. This is a common practice on smaller tech-review channels, that link the products they are reviewing in the description and reference it to the viewers. $1000 may seem much, but remember to low commission rate, and that no product would cost that much, unless there were people willing to pay that price, you just need to direct those people via your affiliate link.

Affiliate marketing is a strong trick to pull because you can have that link in the description of your video for as long as you want, and can be re-placed in the descriptions of future videos, as is the case with cameras in vloggers' content.

This is going to be an early passive income stream, which, to be honest, is going to take time and a big fan-base to earn you over $1000, but once the channel grows and companies start reaching out to you, new affiliations and sponsorships are settled, while the revenue generated by AAM can go directly towards reinvesting.

As you can see, Youtube offers a strong base for any entrepreneur, as all of your monetized assets can be promoted via video streaming, and new passive income streams can be easily established.

As mentioned, we want a solid world of passive income streams, not a single one, while Amazon offers many extremely efficient ways to earn passive income and generate revenue through multiple streams, those streams of income can be centralized towards one single fan base, that will turn into the primary market of all products, and are going to form a solid consumer base, while just having that fan base will generate even more revenue through video monetization and independent sponsorships.

As a last mention, the new GDPR, or General Data Protection Regulation, is expected to hit Youtube pretty hard in the years to follow, and we considered to give you a bit of information on the subject, as the effect it might have on other online businesses is going to be quite significant and is worth taking a look at.

For short, the GDPR is a set of laws issued by the EU in order to keep the

European community's personal data safe over the web, by limiting how much and what type of information can companies store about their customers, such as the name, address, email address, etc. and how each individual customer has to consent for their data to be processed by the company.

The initiative has noble intentions, but as most companies have email lists and work with lots of personal data to better research their customer market, the regulations are less than welcome.

The biggest problem however is how the internet is decentralized, and although the laws would technically only apply in the EU member states, the juridical theory isn't going to work in practice, as many websites are widely spread among the US, the EU, and virtually all countries.

A company could work through the internet in the US and also have customers from the EU, which will automatically have them fall into the fields of the regulation.

Youtube has confirmed after the GDPR initiative was passed in the EU judiciary organs, how the set of laws is going to impact the video platform's algorithms and monetization policy, with new, mandatory standards being implied by the EU through the GDPR laws.

 The article about Youtube's changes can be found online and should also be kept under watch, since as of this writing jurists all over the world are finding new ways of interpretation to some articles in the GDPR.

The Stock Market:

Dividend Paying Stocks

Perhaps you saw this one coming, from books, movies and newspaper headlines, the stock market has been associated with wealth and high-end living since the 90s, with Wall Street being the center of financial attention, through exiting and tense deals massing millions to the brokers.

Success stories circulated all over the 21st century of people who managed to turn their lives around through a good trade and became millionaires soon after, but how realistic are those stories anyway?

To some extent, those stories bear truth within. Professional brokers and trained individuals can make a fortune out of trading, but it is not a get-rich-quick system, trading requires a lot of knowledge about economics and business, and money. To trade stocks, you need to buy stocks, to buy stocks, you need money.

Initially, the stock market wasn't going to be included in this book simply because it is not suitable to the average person, and is very easy to lose money without getting it back, whereas with the other sources of passive income which require some investments, eventually the money will come back, just with no idea when.

Then we figured including the stock market would be suitable to the individuals that start making money through KDP, FBA, or other passive income sources, who will mass a fortune vast enough to invest in stocks that pay their investors back.

The whole goal of this book is to get you into the business world from the comfort of your home, without having to work anymore. Once a five figure system of passive income was established, some will lay back and live off it, while the smartest readers will try to further grow their wealth.

$10,000 / month passively is not the end, it's just the beginning. Once that much money is made, some will indulge themselves in lavish items over the course of a year or two, such as cars, vacations, exotic distractions etc. instead of focusing on turning their wealth towards the next league, which would be around 25k a month.

This requires heavy re-investments in the passive income streams they have already established, as well as new ones, and investments outside the virtual platform, such as real estate, the latter that we will discuss in an upcoming book.

Well, things go about the same way with the stock market, but opposed to KDP, FBA, or other online businesses that can have a huge return on investment over a very short period of time, such as investing $500 to launch your first book or $4000 to start an FBA business, and those activities returning profit in a month, with the stock market the payback rate is significantly lower for the average individual who doesn't want to trade shares.

For anyone who knows anything about the stock market is aware of dividends. For those of you that are unfamiliar about the subject, the stock market juggles with the shares of the company. A share is basically a piece of the company or asset, but a very little one, the money spent on buying those shares goes to the company, who uses that to further develop and grow their company, which ultimately raises its value further-more, resulting in the growth of the shares' prices.

For an established business person, buying $100 million worth of shares, waiting for the company to grow its value over the course of a year, and then sell those shares for $110 million are $10 million made easily, but for the average person the return on investment wouldn't be worth the risk.

Instead, we have the institution of dividends, through which, four times a year, the company pays its shareholders proportionally to their profits. One share could only bring in a few cents, but someone with an impressive portofolio of shares can earn some significant money by simply owning those shares, and re-investing the profits in more shares for the next dividend payout, where more money will be made off those extra shares.

Investing in the stock market in high dividend paying companies can be worth the money, since the dividends coming back to you are a new stream of passive income that can easily be reinvested and the shares that form that stream can always be sold if their value goes up significantly and the investor wants a fresh start with the profits earned.

Investing a portion of the profits you earn after establishing your passive income streams will accumulate over time and form a value mass that could one day bring in an enormous return upon the investment, if the stock prices go up.

The stock market can be a virtual gold mine and nowadays corporations are working on new trading platforms that are more user-friendly and take little commissions if any. A professional trading career can be highly profitable but requires training and investment that are beyond some people.

Generating active income through the internet is more than just simple, anyone with access to the global platform can do it in a variety of ways, as the internet connects billions of people, making it easy for a supplier to reach potential customers in demand, so without further to do, let's get into the active ways you can generate income through the internet.

Freelancing

Most people have probably heard this term before, but the actual meaning is still unclear for many. Freelancing simply refers to people working for themselves rather than for a company, having no boss or schedule, instead relying on their own abilities to reach customers that need their services, and providing those without the interference of companies or employers. While most freelancers do take jobs for companies, they will still go under contract as a freelancing individual, and not an employee.

So who exactly can freelance? The answer to that is, anyone. Most photographers that work privately, without having contact with a photo agency are freelancers, they market themselves, negotiate themselves and get the money for their service for themselves.

The internet provides the best platform for freelancing individuals, allowing anyone to post their services online for free, reaching a massive market for their specific service, especially for jobs that do not require physical contact with the customer.

Voice-over artists, photo and video editors, animators, programmers, life coaches, dating coaches, web designers, writers, all of these services and many more are easily accessible over freelancing platforms such as Fiverr. The freelancer uploads their gig (meaning service) such as " I will create a website for your business" or " I will edit your photos", and gives a brief descriptions of the service, their personal experience in the field, some photos or videos showing examples of the projects he or she has previously done, in order to prove themselves good enough for the customer to hire them for a gig.

The beauty of freelancing through such platforms is the fact that anyone can price their gigs however they like, the way the transaction is done is offered by the website, with the freelancer sending the media files via. their platform and receiving payment the same way, risk free, in exchange for a small commission the platform takes. The biggest advantage these platforms have to offer is the amount of customers you can reach, as the internet literally has billions of users, if only a fraction of those users need a service you offer, and a fraction of those will end up on a freelance platform and only a fraction of those click on your gig and hire you, you'd still have an enormous amount of people to work with.

It's not all that easy however, as there are some main guidelines to follow when setting up your freelancing profile, as these platforms are highly competitive otherwise. Thousands of people offer such services because they are profitable, so you want to make sure whatever business you want to operate in, you must first find your market, and resort to a niche that is not saturated. Meaning that if you are a great bodyweight training athlete, and decide to offer coaching services, do not advertise your product as "sports coach". There are hundreds of sports, and most of them already have tens of freelancers offering their coaching services individually, instead, resort to one single niche in the sports market.

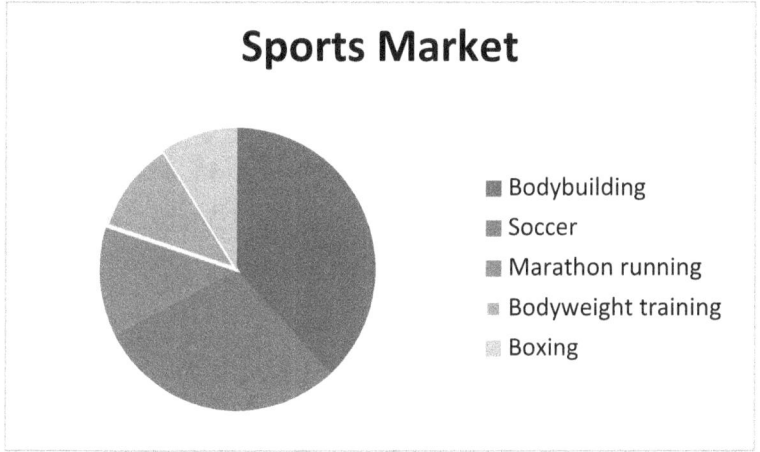

Finding your target audience is key in all internet business, otherwise you might be marketing your service to people uninterested in such gigs, which brings us to the next important factor, marketing.

Such platforms allow users to market their services in exchange for a supplementary fee. These adds do sometimes pay off, but are only advised to freelancers that already generate money, without needing to spend their personal cash and risk not getting the return value back.

The best way for freelancers to market themselves is to set up an attractive profile, making the potential customer to stick to their service, and not check out other fellow freelancers. In order to achieve that, one should use high quality pictures in their gig's description, pictures of themselves doing what they are offering, training, editing, coding, as well as pictures of the end results, such as before and after photos for physical trainers and photo editors, photos of their personal success and greatest achievements in the specific field, etc.

After that, the biggest mistake freelancers make is having poorly written descriptions. Remember that whatever you are selling or offering online, needs a good description. Those 1,000 or 500 words are going to be the cornerstone of your success, those words have to be used well, in order to convince customers to buy your products.

Down below you can see the interface of results when searching for personal training gigs:

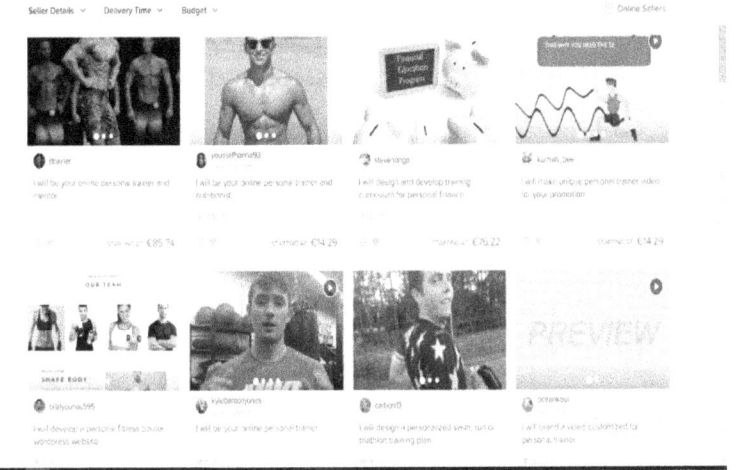

Another added advantage of Fiverr is the analysis system they give you on the seller interface, showing accurate data of impressions, views and clicks, accumulating to a nearly whole market research in the niche through the data collected via your posts.

Software Testing

Countless companies that produce software are on a constant look for people to test their products, analyzing bugs and errors and simply giving them feedback on the issues and places that need improvement.

Such companies are willing to offer great wages to people willing to undergo some training and use their software afterwards as a human error detector.

Even the videogame industry offers to pay people money to play their games prior to their market release. We are not going to go deeper in this topic since each individual will have to do a Google search to find offer around them.

The Millionaire Mindset

Instead of handing out information about the passive income opportunities alone, we've decided to include some insight on the mindset and lifestyle of successful people, in collaboration with Sarmis Wright, author of the Millionaire's Time Management Secrets, available on Amazon.

Setting goals

As most successful people claim, it all started with a dream for them, a dream they wanted to make come true. Setting goals for yourself is the action that leads to more actions towards reaching that goal, otherwise your subconscious will trick you into thinking that what you are currently doing is pointless, and turns that action into a routine, with nothing to motivate it. When we set out goals, and imagine ourselves reaching them, a rush of motivation surges though our bodies that leads towards plans and ideas to make those dreams come true.

Take a few minutes each day, and think about what exactly do you want to achieve, set that one thing clear, regardless of how unrealistic it may initially seem. Yet the answer should be more than fame or fortune, dive into details, and get comfortable with them. A simple exercise to do every day, in fact, you should do it right after you finish reading this section.

Exercise:

- Lay on your couch or bed and make yourself comfortable, have a glass of water, loose fitting clothes, and relax

- Take a deep breath, and close your eyes shut

- Now imagine, imagine yourself in 5 years from now, with your ideal life. Think about your deepest desires, ideals, and simply imagine your perfect life 5 years from now, with as many details as possible. First try to see yourself doing work, regardless of what that means to you in your perfect vision of life, acting, trading stocks, running a corporation, singing in front of thousands of people, imagine the setting, your office, the stage, the set, with every little detail. The clothes you're wearing, the furniture, and most importantly, your face. See in your mind's eye how you are getting work done, maybe crushing a song, signing contracts, writing, and the tools you're using, the perfect microphone, a luxury pen, feel yourself being there.

- Next imagine yourself leaving your workplace, going backstage and catching a breath after the phenomenal concert, leaving the office and getting into your ideal car, as luxurious and slick you as you desire it, see it in detail, with the colors, steering wheel, and hear the engine roar.

- Finally, get the picture of you getting home in your mind. Imagine getting out of the car, and entering your home, a villa, a penthouse, or perhaps just a small house with a garden. See yourself open the door, and watch the furniture closely, focusing on every minor detail you'd want you perfect home 5 years from now to have, perhaps a white piano decorates your living room, or a rare painting adores your walls, as you head towards the couch. Lastly, imagine yourself relaxing, for some, this might mean having a glass of expensive whiskey and smoking a cigar, for others, their relaxation is freshly brewed cup of Arabic coffee, whatever that might be, see it in detail, the shape of the glass or cup, smell the drink you're having, try to taste it.

This is the first part of the exercise, which you should do **right now**, using your imagination. Don't hesitate to go big, if big is what you desire, never doubt your imagination simply because it seems like too much, instead try to accept it.

After doing the first half, the second comes the day after, with the exact same setting, laying comfortably and relaxing, only this time, you will imagine yourself in your perfect life 10 years from now. See what perfection looks for you in twice as much time, without forgetting to go big.

- Start the scenario with you waking up in the morning, where are you? You're in a bedroom or a hotel, what does the furniture look like? See every aspect of your home or room, the colors, the style, and the setting, is it a private room in a luxury hotel, or the bedroom of a mansion with ocean view?
- Next, see if you're alone, do you have a partner, a family perhaps? What do they

look like? Visualize yourself with them, doing an activity, golfing, singing together, perhaps having lunch.

- Ultimately see yourself going to work and getting business done. What are you taking to get there? An exotic sports car? What brand? A high-end SUV or a classic collection car? Is it the one you've been dreaming about? Now what does "work" mean for you? Having an arena full of people waiting for you to get on stage or the top floor office of a multi-million dollar business? See each aspect in the detail, adding all sorts of tweaks to fit your fantasy.

Repeating these two parts continuously will help determine your goal, as some parts and details may change during different days you do this exercise, after a while, each piece will fall into place and form the same vision repeatedly, giving you the exact goal your inner desires dictate.

Incorporating exercises like this in your daily activities requires little to no time, yet the impact it has on your mindset is significant, as each time you imagine this perfect outcome of your life, subconsciously, the image gets burned into your mind, and the words "goal" and "success" will associate themselves to this vision. It is important not to restrict your imagination, as there are limitless scenarios the perfect life can look like.

Psychologically, there has been an ongoing debate about how these goals should be limited, as two groups of specialists claim the contrary to each other. One main group claims that we shouldn't restrict our imagination when it comes to goals, as by raising the standards we vision our future will motivate us to work towards that extravagant vision, and, even if that may be out of reach, by aiming high, even if one does not succeed 100%, achieving just a small portion of what they've dreamt of will already be a success. As an old saying goes "Aim for the moon, so even if you miss you will land on a star."

The other half persuade us towards setting more "realistic" standards and goals, as achieving those is more probable and having an objective accomplished completely will lead to a healthy mind and keep us on track.

We believe in the first group's vision. The ability to let our imagination loose trains creativity over time, a skill essential in the long run, not to mention the consistency with which some pieces of the puzzle can be achieved with. You might not sing for 20,000 people in five years, but singing for just 10,000 is halfway there. These steps that eventually lead to our visions of success will provide us with the required motivation to keep going, unlike setting the goal of singing for 10,000 people, achieving that, feeling satisfied, and going forward on a stagnant level. Always opt for bigger, better and more, never stop setting the bar higher and higher, as achieving parts of it is already a great success, so great that it will keep you motivated to want more and more until it eventually reaches more, with the cycle repeating.

Coming to terms with your expectations is the first step to be taken before focusing on increasing productivity, as it would be absurd to focus on reaching a goal that you haven't set yet. Knowing the direction you're going to is key for not getting lost on the way there, as distractions will occur at every corner.

The next step after setting your goals is to actually ask yourself another question: How do I get there?

No great battle was won without a plan, nor will this one be. It is clear that we need to work hard in order to make our most desired dreams come true, but unless we know how, all of that effort may not contribute at all to the process.

A great example regards wealth, how do we make money? Here comes education, with a variety of books and courses on the rules of money, wealth generating ideas and systems, and investment opportunities.

Another example is of the singer, how do we become famous artists? In this situation education may fall behind practice and talent, no legendary singer performs constantly off-cord. Also the concept of notoriety and showmanship play essential roles in the life of an artist, as a university music teacher won't fill stadiums unless he or she reaches a high level of recognition and appreciation by an audience interested in their specific style.

This is the last issue we're going to address in this section, the problem of "How do I get there?".

Obviously, the answer will vary from person to person, as many will already have a goal set in their mind, and have also started building the road towards that goal, while others will think about this problem for the very first time. Coming to terms with the process needed to make your dreams come true will be the key to ensure that no distraction will affect the process, as it would be absurd for someone dreaming to be one of Shakira's dancers to start by getting waltz lessons. Shakira produces latino music and waltz doesn't really fit the tone.

In terms of wealth, basic education on business and investment opportunities will be enough to put you on track with the necessary information, but for the people seeking more exotic goals, the way to achieve them should be tailored to fit the dream they're pursuing.

As this section comes to an end, all readers are advised to do the exercise scripted above, repeatedly, for a couple of months, and have the final image set in their minds, as in the following we'll focus on the actual ways to increase productivity through time management, and proceeding without the foundation would be foolish.

"All who have accomplished great things have had a great aim, have fixed their gaze on a goal which was high, one which sometimes seemed impossible." —Orison Swett Marden

The Focus and Multitasking Paradox

A true paradox indeed, as we constantly hear people bragging about how efficiently they multitask in order to get more done in less time, so we asked ourselves, is multitasking really that efficient? After all, why wouldn't it be? Simple logic would guarantee that having multiple tasks done at once frees up more space in our daily tasks and thus increases productivity over a shorter period of time, and allows for more tasks to be completed over the time saved through multitasking, right? Wrong.

After doing some research, the results were quite the contrary. Indeed, multitasking is seemingly a good idea, but after going more in-depth, it becomes clear why the contrary is actually the truth. When we multitask, our focus gets divided into two places, task number 1, and task number 2, naturally, one of the tasks, usually the more important one, gets most of our focus, having the secondary task receive only a fraction of our productivity and concentration, making the completion process LESS efficient, while the primary task has less than 100% of our productivity dedicated, as a percentage if allocated to task number 2, thus the primary task also suffers a decrease in productivity and concentration dedicated to it.

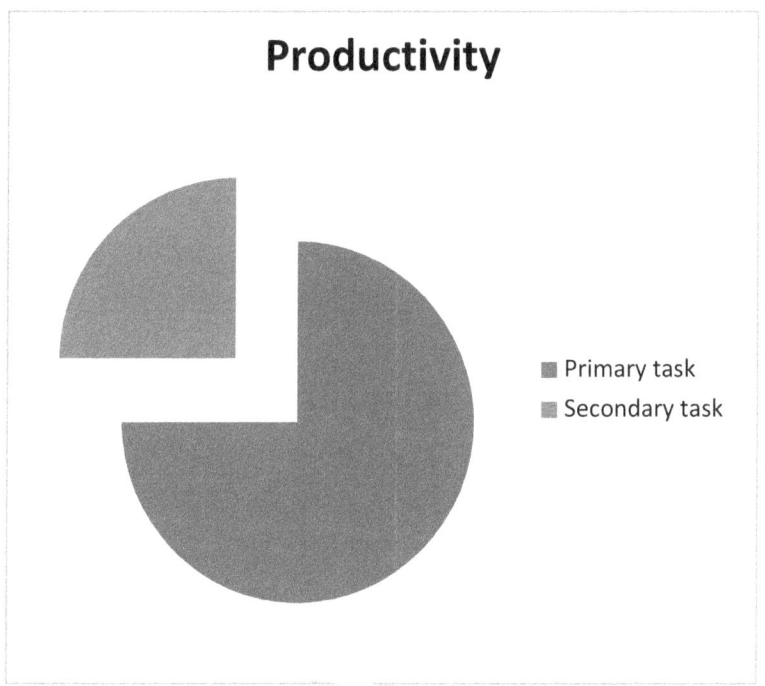

As the primary task requires 100% of one's productivity and focus in order to be completed at 100% efficiency and quality, the more mental resources we dedicate to the secondary task, the more does the primary suffer.

Assuming that the Primary task is essential, while the Secondary task unessential, as trying to multitask two essential ones would be absurd, just imagine working out and attending class at the same time, either one would have to do push-ups while the professor hosts their lecture, or he'd have to go to the gym with the professor in order to get private lectures, absurd, isn't it? Going back to the first idea, one essential and one unessential task, giving studying and organizing a barbeque as the tasks. Having studied at 100% capacity and focus, the whole task would take approximately 2 hours to complete on average, given that we've paid attention in class as well, while organizing the barbeque is about 1 hours' worth of phone calls and discussions, if we take the time to only focus on that.

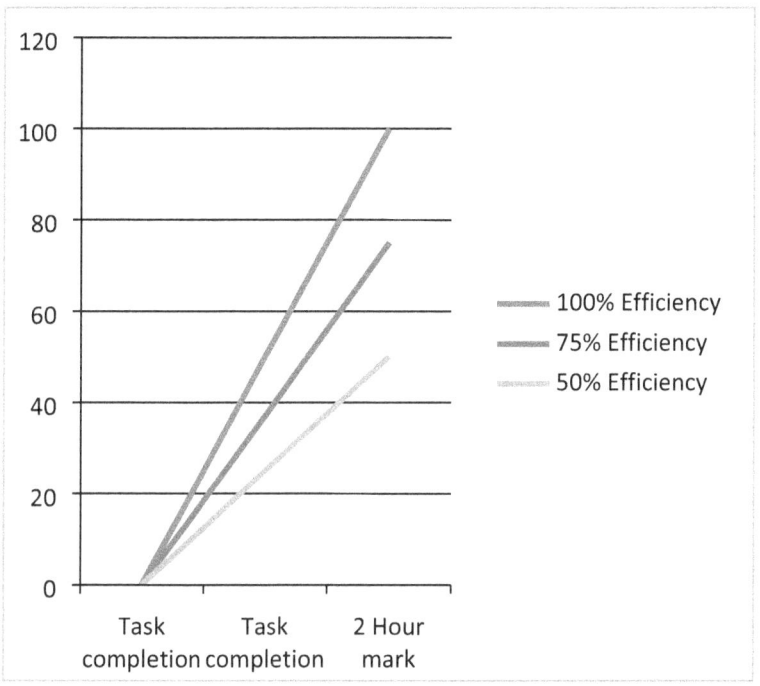

As we can observe, given 2 hours, the less productivity we dedicate to a task, the less we are going to complete from it, ending in the need of dedicating more time towards completion, which contradicts with the need of increasing productivity and time.

If the charts are unclear, think about it more practically, we have a task that requires 2 hours to complete in proportions of 100%, such as studying criminal law, as that's the average time we dedicate to that subject in order to understand and remember the lesson entirely. In the meanwhile, every 20 minutes or so we also dedicate about 5 minutes to answering a phone call or responding to a text message, adding up to 30 minutes spent on the phone, making our study session 2 hours and 30 minutes in order to get done with both tasks, so far so good, but now take into consideration how every phone call or text message interrupts our focus, and by the time we properly get it back in order to keep studying at high capacity, we get another interruption by a message or call. Not only are we losing potential time, as the 2 hour study session turned into 2 and a half, but the most damaging part to our efficiency and productivity is the effect it has on our product quality.

The product is the actual remembering and perhaps notes of the lesson, however through the constant loss of focus, nor our attention whilst reading, nor the notes we took were not of average quality, but worse, while our goal is to output the highest quality work in the least amount of time. Not only that, but by multitasking in between an essential and an unessential task, both suffered in terms of quality and ALSO TIME. If we were to dedicate those 2 hours to exclusively studying, first of all the quality of the action would be much higher, and secondly, leaving the barbeque related conversations for later would allow for a solid 20 minutes of time dedicated strictly to organizing the barbeque efficiently, by focusing solely on reaching out to guests and delegating certain tasks to others. Multitasking may be efficient in terms of doing two small, unessential tasks at once, which can suffer quality-wise, as long as they do not affect the time dedicated to them. A great example would be taking out the trash while going after the groceries, and we call this a great example because this is such an unimportant and average situation that multitasking actually becomes viable, as the quality of the action of taking out the trash or bringing in the groceries cannot actually suffer and you save yourself about 2 minutes.

Multitasking is NOT the way to go about considerable tasks, but rather small activities that are hard to screw up and require little to no focus to complete. The actual ability to multitask is a great characteristic of the efficient person, but not because of the actual use of multitasking, but because it suggests high focus and intelligence skills, which ultimately become useful in the professional and essential activities needed towards success.

> *"Fucking two things up at the same time isn`t multitasking"*
>
> *-- Dick Masterson*

Task Priority

Finding and setting certain levels of importance to the tasks listed for a period of time is an incredible form of organization, having the added advantage of knowing when certain essential tasks have to be taken care of, scheduling the rest accordingly. Since most of the following pages revolves around tasks and efficiency, we are going to be using an example list, with the tasks the author had on his list during most of the time spent in Law school.

- Go to the gym
- Attend the courses
- House work
- Study
- Business

Looking at the importance of the tasks, we can observe how we have a mix of essential and unessential tasks, judged through a subjective filter.

Going to the gym was an absolutely essential task, at least for the author, since working out has been playing a key role since his early teenage years, but from an objective point of view, it shines more towards and unessential category. Certain character defining tasks that for some are an extreme necessity, can be an absolutely inessential activity, having each individual judge which tasks are and which are not essential.

Course attendance was without a doubt essential, regardless of the subjectivity or objectivity of the filter we're determining it through, as the courses are the very essence of going to college, especially when the diploma obtained plays a solid role in the persons' future. Also, the law courses teach important protocols and systems that are undoubtedly helpful when it comes to business, so the lessons were also essential for the desired goal of the individual.

Next we have house work, which was the general term used for the childhood chores that needed to be completed, such as cooking, cleaning, laundry, etc. and the note in the list meant one or two of those tasks. As a characteristic, the activities were unessential, as the impact they played towards achieving high standard goals was almost irrelevant, yet, at least twice a week those tasks became necessary for a healthy space and body.

Studying was a complimentary task to the overall niche of academic education, yet, it did not come right after class, and we'll get to that in a minute.

Lastly we have business, which for the author meant studying and investing in intellectual property, such as video courses, books, and design. For sure essential, leaving this task last had a very powerful reasoning behind it, one that will make sense in the next paragraph discussing how the list should be assembled based on practicality and priority.

Further dissecting the structure of the list, we have a full day, along with the unessential tasks left out from the list, in order to present a better understanding of what and how should follow each task you write on your to-do-list, in the authors' words:

"Gym was incredibly important to me, almost as important as college, so I had to

find a way to pursue both. I had classes usually around noon or earlier in the morning, and I totally hated going to the gym in the afternoon or evening when it's most crowded, so the only choice I had was to wake up 3 hours prior to class, with my backpack and gym bag ready from the night before to make it in time. Usually I woke up, brewed a black coffee quickly, slammed it as if I were drinking tequila, got dressed really quick and I went straight to the gym, eating the banana on the way. I had a variety of gyms around me, but I was somewhat forced to pick the one nearest to my apartment, as the time spent going there and getting back was valuable. After completing my workouts, which got more intense than in the summer, having no time to waste, I hurried back home, made myself scrambled eggs and showered while the eggs were cooling. While eating I'd do my social media check, I was a teenager after all, then got dressed ASAP and rushed to class. Whenever I had extra time left before having to leave the house I would load or unload the dishwasher, clean my shoes, or other activities I'd have to complete anyway later in the day or week. After class I would usually make my way home and slam in a protein shake while doing something I'd regard as a chore, such as meal prep, laundry or just cleaning a room or two in the apartment, only then I had lunch. Having my energy levels refilled, and cup of coffee I'd make after lunch, it was study time. I hated giving myself time limits, and except for the gym, where I had no other choice, I would study until I felt confident in the day's lesson and a quick recap of the previous one, usually taking an hour or two. When most people talk about law school they associate it with a lot of reading and studying, which is true, but paying very close attention in class helps enormously. After studying, I would have a quick break, after which I was ready to finish my duties by offering all of my remaining productivity and time to improve my intellectual property I had published on different platforms, as well as starting new projects, recording material, editing it, writing details and plans, with the sole purpose of seeing results the following weeks. I would always set checkpoints, such as earning a specified amount for 2 months in a row, after which I stepped my game up, and invested more time and money towards the business. I had a certain checkpoint for each day as well, such as edit a half-hour course, or record 3 courses worth of material, and whenever I managed to complete the task in less time than I thought it would take, I'd ALWAYS do extra. When I was finally done with my tasks, the feeling that rushed through my body was incredible, I felt like I could accomplish anything, and any extra time I had left before bedtime, and yes, I set myself bedtimes, based on the time I had to get up the next day, was entertainment. Having friends over, watching a series, etc. after all I was human, and needed recreation. Activities such as parties or late nights in bars were no strangers to me, but only when I could fit them in my schedule, whether by doing the next day's house work the day before, or simply having no classes the next day, but balance was the key to an efficient schedule. Ultimately before going to sleep, I had a routine I found crucial for my life to work the way it did, hypnosis, something I encountered years before when I was doing magic tricks in high-school. Hypnosis was such a game-changer in terms of productivity, waking up feeling fresh, energy and motivation that I couldn't leave it out of this book, as the role it played throughout my life was irreplaceable. The last section will be dedicated to resting, and I will include my full guide to self-hypnosis, along with three different script blueprints and two fully written script, once of which was specially written for the readers looking to drastically improve their productivity and live every minute of their life, feeling energized even with less than 8 hours of sleep per night."

Based on what you've just read, tasks should be prioritized depending on their importance and practicality in time, as some tasks cannot be done whenever we desire to do so, instead are set for a specific time, as was the case with the classes in the authors' daily routine, and as other tasks are preferred to be done in a specific time window, without being necessarily tied to that, as was going to the gym in the morning in the paragraph above, first things first, you need to determine the importance and practicality of the tasks you set on your list, and the order it's easiest and most efficient to go about them. Experiment with different orders to complete tasks in, in order to find out which system works best for you, however a solid recommendation is to fix the essential tasks that are set for a place and time, and start building around those, such as a job or education.

"To change your life, you need to change your priorities." -- Mark Twain

www.ingramcontent.com/pod-product-compliance
Lightning Source LLC
Chambersburg PA
CBHW070417220526
45466CB00004B/1443